KNOT TYING (

LEARN HOW TO TIE 35+ KNOT WITH THIS KNOT TYING KIT FOR BEGINNERS TO LEARN BASIC AND SOPHISTICATED KNOT TYING TECHNIQUES WITH THE AID OF PICTURES

BY

GEORGE M. GRAY

Table of Contents

INTRODUCTION

The knot has always been one of those key skills done outdoor that inexperienced people take for granted. However, seasoned nature lovers have had enough failures and success to know that there are wrong and right knots for certain jobs.

A good knot can save lives when it comes to survival, first aid, and when working at heights or in the water. However, you should know how to tie it. So make sure you know what to do with your rope the next time you delve into nature.

PART 1

WHAT IS A KNOT

A knot is a type of fixation or joint that is made by entangling one or more rope or other elastic material. After tightening the knot, it should stand on its own. A hitch is slightly different. Similar to a knot, but it usually involves something else like a stick, ring, post, or sometimes another rope. Correctly tied, the hitches can hold their place, or they can slide, depending on the hook (hitch) you choose. Lashing is like a hitch, but it's a little more complicated. Fastening (lashing) involves using a rope or similar material to secure two or more things together. To simplify all this, the knot is just a rope tied. A hitch is a rope attached to a body; A tie is a rope that holds multiple things together.

ROPE KNOT TERMS

There are specific terminologies to describe the parts of the node while attaching it. Common parts of the node are described and described below.

Tying the knot terminology instructions

Bight: any part of the rope between the ends. The bight is also used to denote a curved section of the rope within a tied knot.

Crossing Point: The place where the ropes intersect in a ring.

Elbow: two or more rings that are very close to each other.

Ring/loop: The bight becomes a ring at the intersection of the two ropes. If the end of work is crossed above the foot line, then it is an overhead loop. It is a hidden ring if the end of the work is running in the lower right side.

Working end: The active end used to knot the knot.

Standing/Permanent end: The end is not used to tie a knot. The part of the unused rope is called the permanent part.

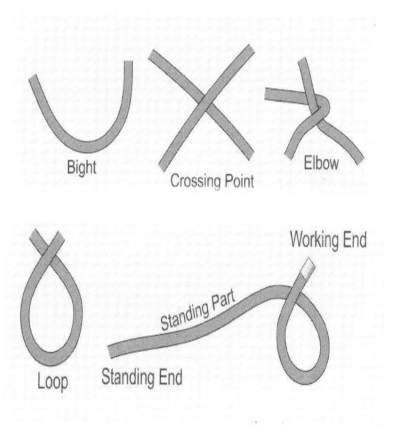

Bight

Crossing Point

Elbow

Working End

Standing Part

Loop   Standing End

TYPES OF ROPE

Ropemakers seem happy to confuse us with names and unusual multi-syllable science. Let us try cutting it a little.

POLYESTER

Polyester is also known as terylene or dacron, which is the material that makes up most of the "ordinary" cable and line. It is resistant to mold and UV rays, sinks in water, and comes in a variety of constructions:

❖ **3-strand pre-strands:** can be tied in the normal way, although it is a good idea to use 4 or 5 strands instead of 3 used on natural fiber ropes. "Pre-stretch" refers to an additional disk that moves during rope manufacture making it more suitable for rope balls and bells. So important that, can you imagine the tone that could result from the use of a rubber cord? The drawback of this construction is that it can deviate, so it is not usual to use it as a sheet.

❖ **Plaited Pre-Stretched**: It comes in all sizes from 1mm to top, but is generally not used above 8mm as it takes over the braided rope (see below). It behaves well and finds its use as lacing, messengers, etc in smaller sizes and halyards in larger sizes. But it can't be tied easily, so you need to hold or grab it.

❖ **Braided rope:** these are the most used objects for sheets. Available in a variety of construction and exterior finishes, starting around 5mm. The type we include is the outer matte braid over the heart of the braid. It's pluggable, with some practice, but each manufacturer uses a slightly different construction, so you should follow the proper instructions for that rope.

POLYPROPYLENE

Slightly more elastic than polyester, polypropylene floats in water and will degrade over time under ultraviolet radiation. It usually comes in the form of 3 strands, except for the skating/rescue ropes that are braided, and the main diversification is the way the materials are incorporated into the rope. I don't pretend to understand the details of the process, but I can feel some results:

❖ **Staple Spun Polyprop**: Cheap hair stuff you can get in blue, orange, or white that can be seen on farms, fishing boats, and construction sites. Except for moorings, which are often not seen on yachts

* **Mono / Polypropyl Monofilament:** Complicated like polyester, but, as mentioned above, decomposes over time and can dissolve if raised around an anchor point. How to tell one about the other? Put it in the water, hold it on one end! If it floats it is polypropylene. It's not a bad rope, but be aware of its limits and keep looking for the brittleness that develops with the age-like fragments that appear in the outer fibers.

* **Hemp strings:** now they are cheaper than the natural ones that replace them and they behave better and for a longer time. It comes in a smooth finish, which looks good when new, but is somewhat flexible, not particularly durable, but more sheet-friendly. The more solid varieties, for example, "Leoflex" or "Spunflex", look slightly shiny when new, but last longer, usually 10 to 15 years, extend much less

and are cheaper. Visitors can see it used in Flagstaff (!) - Currently 6 years old and show no signs of deterioration.

NYLON

Nylon is very flexible and is therefore used for anchor ropes and tow lines. Its expansion makes it very good for storing energy, but if it breaks that energy, it is released very quickly.

HEMP, SISAL, COIR, MANILA

Natural fiber ropes were the choice of poor sailors, but few are more expensive now. Therefore, its use is difficult to justify, except for decorative purposes or defenses, where coir fibers are still useful.

ROPE CARE

Now if your rope is an expensive, non-expendable type used in critical security situations like climbing, landing, sailing, and rescue operations then you need to take care of it and pay attention to its maintenance.

HOW TO CARE FOR A ROPE

Keep your rope off the ground. Keep the rope up so that dirt, grease, chemicals, and various debris cannot touch it. These things can damage the fibers of the material and weaken the string. For climbing ropes, when you use them outdoors, it's best to put them on a tarp so they stay off the ground.

Keeping the rope off the ground when not in use also prevents people from slipping, which can damage and grind dirt into fibers.

Keep the rope away from the sun and excessive heat. Although the most advanced and modern cables are processed to avoid ultraviolet rays, you still want to store the rope out of sunlight when not in use. Excessive heat can also weaken the rope, so do not store it in a warm cabin or attic.

Clean your rope as needed. If the cord becomes dirty, wash it with cold water and mild soap. Rinse with cold water to remove soap. Hang up and let the air dry. Do not put the rope in the sun to dry or use heaters to speed up the process. Make sure the rope is completely dry before winding and hanging it.

Check the cable from time to time for damage. After using your cable, do a quick damage check. According to REI, you want to find the following defects:

* ❖ Are there very fuzzy areas?
* ❖ Do you see or feel cuts?
* ❖ Do you see or feel flat spots?
* ❖ Does the rope look stiff?
* ❖ Can you see the core of the rope?
* ❖ Do you see the discoloration from the sun and/or chemical exposure?

If the answer is yes to any of these questions, it is likely to retract the cord.

Replace the climbing rope regularly. As a climber, his rope is usually the main thing that prevents him from falling to his death. As a result, you need to make sure that the rope is shaped like a ridge. Manufacturers of climbing ropes set removal times for your climbing rope so that you do not use a potentially dangerous rope

When to replace a rope:

- ❖ After falling with heavy loads or other damage: immediately
- ❖ Frequent use (weekly): one year or earlier
- ❖ Regular use (few times per month): 1-3 years
- ❖ Accidental use (once a month): 4-5 years
- ❖ Rare use (1-2 times a year): 7 years

To keep track of how often you use a climbing rope, it is recommended to label the rope with a sign at one end (for example, "rope A"), then record the dates you used it in a logbook.

What do you do with a retired climbing rope? Do not discard it. Although it is no longer suitable for important safety activities like climbing, you can still use it for business on camping trips (such as forged fabrics) or around the house as a washing line.

HOW TO WRAP YOUR ROPE TO STORE IT

When you don't use your rope, you'll want to store it off the ground again to keep it clean and out of harm's way. Here's how to wrap the rope for easy storage and loosening.

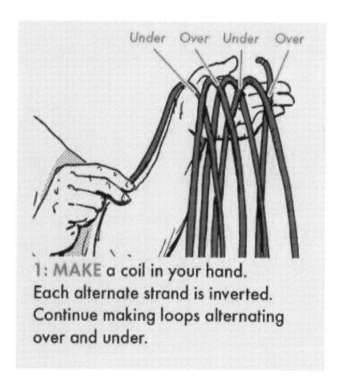

1: MAKE a coil in your hand.
Each alternate strand is inverted.
Continue making loops alternating
over and under.

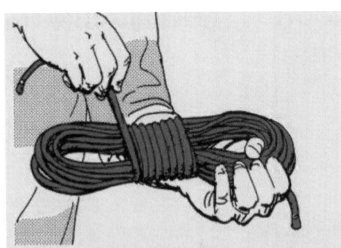

2: WHEN you have about two or three feet of rope left, wrap it around the coil several times.

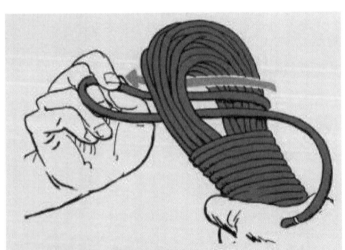

3: MAKE a bite (a bend) in the remaining end and pass it through the coil.

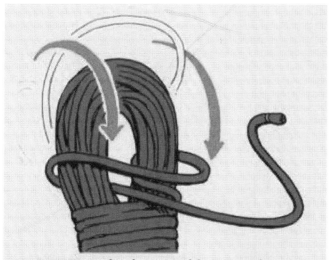

4: SPREAD the bite and bring it down over the coil.

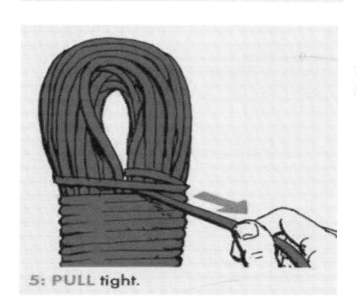

5: PULL tight.

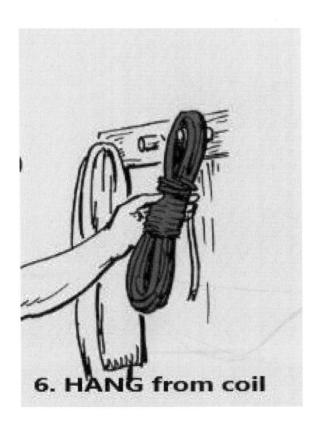

6. HANG from coil

PART 2

BASIC KNOTS

SQUARE KNOTS

The square knot is a classic to tie lines and knots. If you tie two ropes together to make a longer rope or a bundle of firewood for transportation, the square knot is the winner. It is safer and more stable than the granny knot, which everyone may be familiar with as part of tying their shoes.

How to tie a square knot:

You can tie a solid square knot by wrapping one rope from right to left, then down the other, then tying it again in the opposite direction, from left to right, then below. You will know that you did it right when the end of work and the end of each rope are next to each other (without making a "cross" like a granny knot).

CLOVE HITCH

Clove Hitch is an easy knot to tie, and fastens to a tree or pole quickly, but slides when worn alone, without any other support knot.

How to tie a nail/clove hitch:

To create a nail/clove hook on a tree, make a rope loop around the tree. Then make another loop and slide the free end of the rope under the second loop before attaching. To tie this to a column or stake, just create a loop at the free end of the rope and move it over the electrode. Then make another loop just like the first loop. Place the second ring on the column (just above the first ring) and fasten the hitch.

BOW LINE

The bending line (bowline) creates a loop at the end of a rope that cannot shrink or expand. This knot is often marked and illustrated with a rabbit poem coming out of the hole, jumping in front of the tree, going behind the tree, and descending into the original hole.

How to tie a neckline:

Repeat the top end of the long line. Slide the end of the line action up to and around the loop behind the line. Then pass the end of the work down through the original loop, keeping the shape of the second loop you create, which becomes the arc (bowline) loop. Once the "rabbit" returns to the bottom of the hole, pull the "tree" up to tighten the neckline/bowline.

FIGURE 8 KNOTS

The eighth shape is often used for climbing and sailing, an easy-to-use single-thread "stopper" knot that prevents the rope from slipping through something like a washer.

The eight-knot shape creates a stopper wherever you need one on the rope, although the steps are steps you need to take to create another different knot.

How to tie figure eight:

To connect the number eight, also known as the flamenco curve, simply turn the free end of a line on yourself to form a loop. Continue below and around the line, and finish the knot by passing the end of the work down through the original loop.

THE SHEET BEND

The sheet bend is a nice one as well, although technically it is a "curve", a type of knot that connects a rope to another. It's the best curve to tie different types of materials or join different rope thicknesses. This knot binds up to streaks or materials that usually cannot be tied due to diameter differences.

How to tie the paper curve:

To create a sheet bend, fold the thick or slippery "J" rope (like a hook). Then, pass the other rope through the shape of the hook from the back, wrap it around the entire hook at once, and then insert the smaller line between you and the other rope. If the rope has the same diameter and texture, then the curve of the blade is actually like a square knot. To tie a sheet bend with a tarp or fabric, collect, compress and form the material "J", then wrap the rope through and around "J".

TWO HALF HITCHES

You can use half of the hooks to secure a line for trees or columns or to secure the line to yourself as if you were tying up the truck driver's obstacle. The half hook is easy enough to fasten and I often use it to fasten the covers to shelter or hang hammocks.

How to tie half hooks:

After winding the rope around the tip of the foot and through the inner ring created to create the first half of the first traction joint, twist the line in the same way again to make the half of the second traction joint. Pull it well and you should have half hitches, one sitting next to the other. If you want additional security, you can tie a knot over the head at the end of the card to prevent half of the hooks from slipping.

TAUT LINE HITCH

The tight line knot takes the place of the slide to tighten or loosen the loop on a line (such as the tent line). This knot remains narrow as long as there is tension on the "narrow" side of the loop.

How to tie a knotted line:

To tie a tight line hurdle, create a loop by winding a solid and fixed object such as a tree or tent stake. With the free end of the rope, wrap the mainline twice inside the loop. Then put the free end of the chain on the two turns, wrap it around the mainline, and draw the end of the tag with the loop you just created. The cinch wraps uptight. Pull the foot line and the hook line should be connected to the line loading line.

FISHERMAN'S KNOT

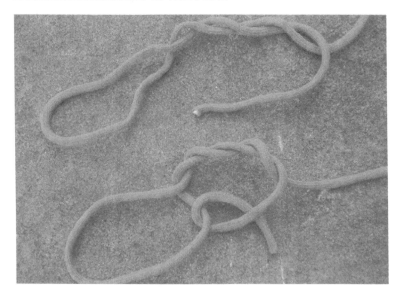

True to his name, the hunter knot is practically good only for use with the fishing line.

How to tie a fisherman knot:

Slide the free end of the line over or around the object to be secured, for example, through the hook's eye. Then turn the free end of the line around the other from the line about five to six times. Pass the free end of the line through the triangular hole next to the locked object, then pass the free end of the line through the large loop you just created by passing through the small triangle. If you are tying this to the fishing line, spit on the line before tightening it to lubricate it so that the friction does not cause thermal damage to the line. Tighten the knot, trim any extra lines, and enjoy your day fishing.

WATER KNOT

The water knot secures belts, flat belts, and most types of belts together.

How to tie a water knot:

To tie the water knot, start with a loose knot at the end of the tape. Attach the other strip in the opposite direction to reflect the path of the knot on the first strip. Take the ends of the two belts and tie the knot. That's it, it's very simple and very powerful.

ROLLING HITCH

Rolling Hitch adds leg to the existing line. This knot is the primary node behind a tight line knot, but it can be added to any existing line. The winding hitch has often been used historically to connect more dogs to the main dog sled line.

How to tie a rolling obstacle:

Wrap the free end of the rope around the main rope to create a half hook. Make a second half of a second hurdle and then turn the whole knot to end with one last obstacle on the other side of the starting position.

PRUSIK KNOT

Prusik knot creates a loop that can be used ascending or descending. This "slip-and-grip" knot can also be useful to add a loop to the rope when neither end of the rope is free.

How to tie a Prusik knot

To tie Prusik you will need a short rope and a separate long rope. Tie the bow on the short rope that is fixed with hard knots like the square knot. Now wrap the loop around the long rope three times, making sure that each wrap falls on the long rope. Slide the short rope loop under itself and pull it tightly. As long as there is weight in the ring, Prusik will hold on to the long rope. You can also slide Prusik up or down the long-chain by removing the loop weight and pushing the bars up or down.

TIMBER HITCH

The wooden traction joint attaches a rope to an object to carry or act as support.

How to tie a wooden hook:

To create a wooden obstacle, all you have to do is pass the free end of the rope around the object, like the log, that you intend to pull. Then, wrap the end of the mark around the inside of the loop you created four or five times. After tightening the wooden traction joint so that the four or five turns are stretched to the body, the continuous tension on the traction joint will remain in the sitting position.

THE BLOOD KNOT

This little jewel on the fishing line is used to secure two lines together (fix a broken line or join leaders and nipples).

How to tie a blood knot:

The blood knot will start by overlapping the two lines and wrapping one free tip around the other line five or six times. Swipe the free end between the two lines. Turn the other line the same number of times (five or six), then place the free end backward between the two lines in the direction opposite to the other free end of the line. If you are using a fishing line, spit it out to reduce friction damage.

HARNESS MEN

This cunning knot allows you to place a loop on a line along the rope when none of the ends of the line is free to tie the bow, and you have not heard from me, but the man's belt is great for cheating. Tug of war

How to tie a man's belt:

Collect some slack on the line and the loop so that part of the line passes through the middle of the loop. Hold the side of the loop and drag it across the distance between the line in the middle and the other side of the loop. Tighten the new ring, then pull the line to secure the knot to the men's belt. This knot can slip if there is no constant tension in the newly created ring, so hold something in the loop to hold it.

CARRICK BEND

This alternative to square knot secures two cords securely and is easy to loosen from the square knot.

How to tie a Carrick curve:

To tie Carrick Bend, form a loop with the end of the rope. Slide the free end of the other rope under the first loop, then again at the bottom as shown in the picture. Slide the free end through the loop that passes under itself, and pull both ends to tighten.

TRUCKER HITCH

You do not have to be a truck driver to use this powerful hitch. The unique advantage of the truck driver hitch is that it gives you a unique mechanical advantage to line pull. Although tying this issue is a little complicated, it's worth it if you need to tighten the lines as much as possible before securing them; I use it all the time to tie the covers or secure variable loads.

How to tie the truck driver hitch:

Begin by tying a knot in Figure 8 to a line loop. Then slide the free end of the line around or through what ties the rope, before passing the line through the loop. Then fasten the working end and fasten the free end with two connectors, just below the loop.

SHEEPSHANK

This knot looks like a half magic trick, half a practical knot, but it shortens the line without cutting it. This knot keeps our long ropes in one piece, despite our miscalculated calculus.

How to tie a lamb:

To tie the sheepshank, fold the rope to the new length you need. Create a half hitch on one end of the continuous rope and drop it over the adjacent loop. Make a half hitch on the other end, place it over the ring next to it, and then tighten everything slowly.

TRIPOD KNOT

The tie-leg mount is commonly used in shelters and for carrying camping gear, such as a pot over a fire.

How to connect a tripod:

Start by choosing three poles of approximately the same length and thickness and lay them on the floor next to each other. Attach the nail hook to one of the terminal supports, then wrap all the supports four, five, or six times. Now, wrap the line between posts, twice between each one, and work toward the original knot or link you tied. Finish the tie by tying the end of the sticker to the end of the original knot. Extend the tripod legs and use them in the camp to get something useful.

SQUARE STRAP

Square Lashing was used to build everything from camping chairs to towers and bridges, but you can also use it to secure two poles together.

How to tie a square tie:

Attach the clove hitch to one of the poles near where the two posts intersect. Then, wrap your line around the intersection of the poles, passing under the bottom pole and above the top pole. Roll with these covers five or six times. Then, wrap between the poles, and press the old casings to tighten it. Finally, use a square knot to tie the free end of the rope to the free end to tie a nail that started this entire beating.

PART 3

BOATING KNOTS

The rope knot, boating, and sailing go hand in hand. Most of the knot goes back to the early days of sailing. For example, the Buntline hitch was used to secure the buntline at the foot of the sails on square deck boats.

ANCHOR BEND

Anchor Bend or Anchor Hitch is the node generally used to attach a line to the anchor. The free end must be secured with a fist on the support line for a permanent and secure knot. One side of Double Fisherman's is a good backup node for this and any other node.

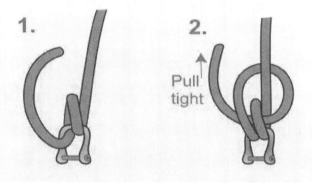

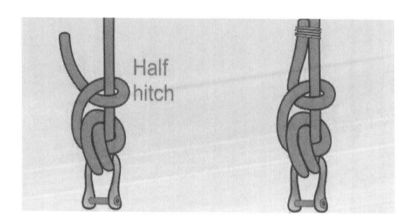

INSTRUCTIONS

✓ Take two turns around the constraint, leaving the turns open.

✓ Pass the free end behind the support line and pass the free end through the first few turns and pull strongly.

✓ Now tie the half hook around the foot line and pull firmly.

✓ Grab the free end or tie the knot to the end of a long mark and tie the back knot like the half of the double hunter knot with the end of the mark around the right side.

ASHLEY BEND

This useful knot works well on a variety of materials, including bungee cords. Because it will accept pulling any of the four directions to its ends, it can be used to form the center

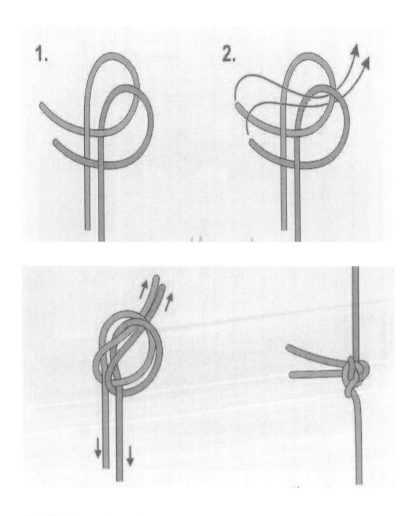

INSTRUCTIONS

✓ Form a loop at the end of the rope,
   preparing to tie it to the Overhand knot.

✓ Take the end of the second rope and feed through the first loop, making its loop to be tied in the Overhand knot.

✓ Complete both overlapping knots, taking into account feeding the ends

✓ Pull all sides to tighten.

CARRICK BEND

Carrick Bend is an excellent knot for joining two strands, especially those with large diameter ropes and cable ties. It extends significantly under load and although it may lose its symmetrical shape, it remains safe. The ends of the label can be attached to the permanent lines for added safety.

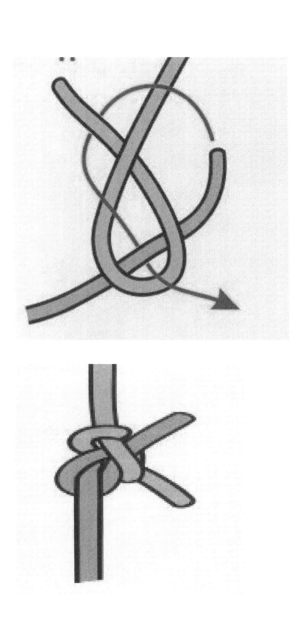

INSTRUCTIONS

✓ Form a primary loop with a larger rope (a white rope in the illustration) and place the loop above and across the end of the second rope's work.

✓ Remember the sequence: up, down, up, down, up, and pass the end of work for the second rope around the first loop and follow the sequence.

✓ The limbs come out on either side of the knot. The knot loses its beautiful symmetry when stretched.

✓ The ends should be attached to the foot parts of the strings are large.

COMMON WHIPPING

A common whip is a knot tied to the end of the rope to prevent the end from breaking apart. The benefit of a common tie knot is that it is fairly easy to knit and no tools are required. However, the knot is more suitable for temporary use or in decorative ropes, as it is known to slip easily from the rope. It is preferably used on a natural fiber rope and tied with a natural rope, providing maximum friction to the knot to fix it at the end of the rope. When it comes to synthetic ropes, it is best to wrap with duct tape and then heat the ends to the melting point to merge the strings.

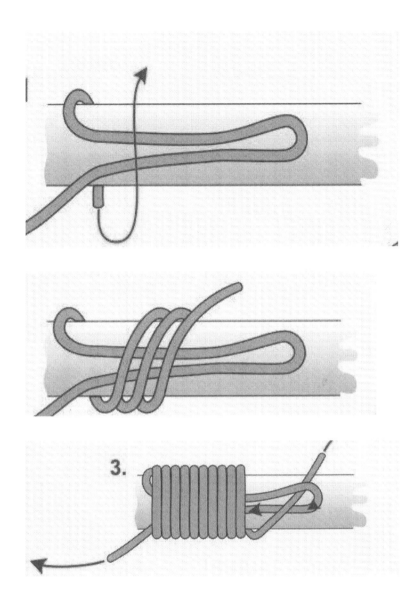

3.

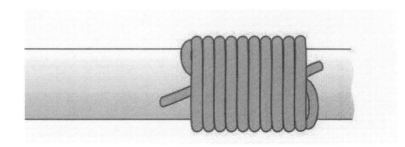

INSTRUCTIONS

- ✓ Place the rope along the rope and bight back along the rope. Note that the rope should be whipped a short distance (one-and-a-half times) from its end.
- ✓ Start wrapping the rope around the twine and then tightly wrapping them. Wrap it until whipping is 1.5 times wider than floss.
- ✓ Pass the end of the rope through the bight. Gently pull the tip of the rope until the cavity and end of work are below the whip (note: it is usually necessary to maintain tension at the end of the work to prevent the hollow from pulling out completely,

otherwise the whip will collapse.) Cut the thread with the edges of the lash to give the end of the rope a final look.

DOUBLE BOWLINE KNOT

Double Bowline Line is also known as Round-Turn Bowline and it is often called Water Bowline. It's a classic Bowline knot with two overlapped loops, or with an extra wrap around the bore. The extra strength and durability of the Bow Bowline make it well suited for tough activities and heavy manipulation.

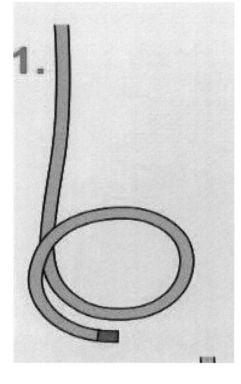

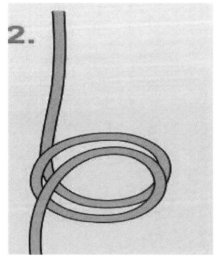

3.

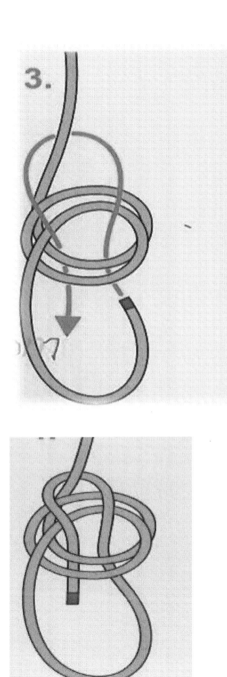

INSTRUCTIONS FOR TYING A DOUBLE BOW KNOT

- ✓ Place the rope on your left hand with the free end hanging. Form a small loop on the line in your hand.
- ✓ Repeat to create a second small loop under the first.

- ✓ Bring the free end and pass through the small rings from the underside (the rabbit comes out of the hole).
- ✓ Roll the line around the standing line and review it through the two rings (around the tree and return the hole).
- ✓ Tighten the knot by pulling the free end while maintaining the standing line.

HALLYARD HITCH

Halyard Hitch makes up a very small knot making it a good option for tying a halyard, shackle, or even a small loop. Once tightened or placed under load, it is almost impossible to loosen the halyard knot and will likely require cutting if necessary. A similar and effective knot is the Buntline hitch.

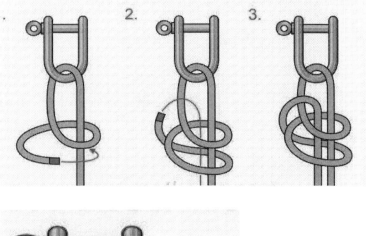

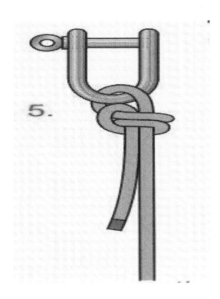

INSTRUCTIONS FOR TYING THE HALYARD NODE KNOT

- ✓ Pass the end of the rope through the cuff and turn around the standing line.
- ✓ Take a second round around the standing line under the first corner.
- ✓ Place the end of the rope back on top of the knot and feed the end through the two loops you just created.
- ✓ Pull the end to tie the knot, and then pull the support line to fix the knot to the shackle.

ZEPPELIN CURVE

The Zeppelin Bend knot, also known as the Rosendahl Bend knot, is used to join two ropes. It is an easy knot to tie, very safe, and jam-proof.

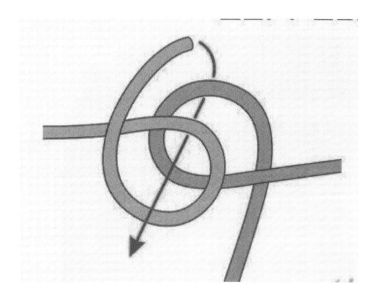

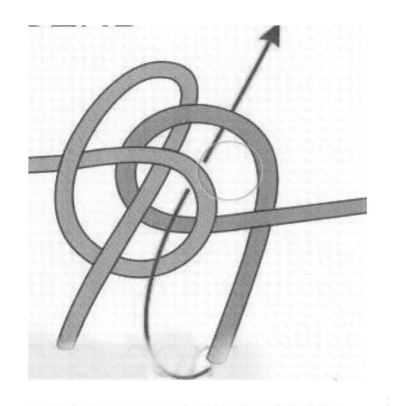

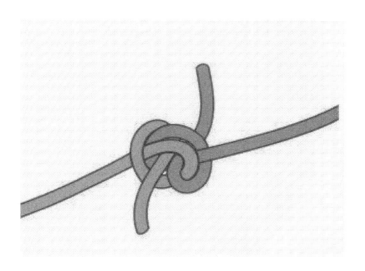

INSTRUCTIONS

- ✓ An easy way to start the Zeppelin knot is to form a "6" with one rope with the running line down, and a "9" formation with the other rope with the race line. Then place 6 partially above 9.
- ✓ Take the end of 6 and turn it on through opening 9 and 6.
- ✓ Repeat with end 9 in the opposite direction, through slot 6 and slot 9.
- ✓ Pull the ends tightly.

ROLLING HITCH

A very safe and easy way to tie a rope with a rope. The knot is securely fastened in the direction of the standing line. The rolling hitch is safer than the clove hitch when attaching a rope to a pole or something else.

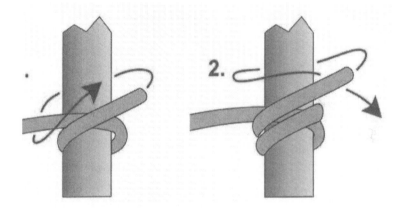

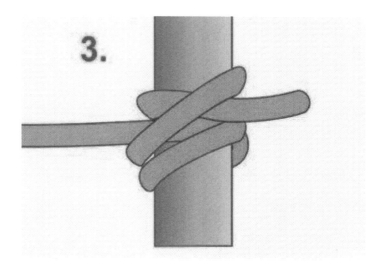

INSTRUCTIONS FOR TYING

- ✓ Wrap the end of the line around an object. Repeat, cross the standing line again.
- ✓ Wrap a third time around the body, but wrap it over the standing line so you don't cross it.
- ✓ Slide the free end under the last warp and pull firmly.

MOORING HITCH

Good temporary knot. It can be edited quickly by pulling on the free end. The mooring knot is quickly fastened under load but is immediately disarmed by drawing on the end of the mark. It can be securely attached to anything or anywhere along the rope so you can reach and drop it without getting off your horse or exiting your boat.

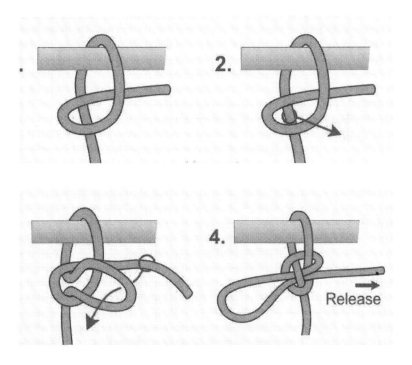

GUIDELINES

- ✓ Wrap around the prism, then repeat the free end coming out of the loop inside (leave the free end longer than shown).
- ✓ Take the standing line and pass a clip through the loop.
- ✓ Get part of the free end (but not the end) and pull the track through the new loop.
- ✓ Pull the knot by pulling down on the standing line. Free the knot by dragging the free end.

PART 4

CLIMBING KNOT

ALPINE BUTTERFLY BEND

The Butterfly Bend, as it is also known, is a method of attaching two ropes derived from the alpine butterfly loop, or the tie of a Lehmann loop, except that it is tied to the ends of two ropes. Another way to knit this knot (which differs in shape from the method described here) is to tape or hold the ends of the two strings temporarily, then proceed to tie the alpine butterfly. When the knot is complete, loosen the ends, and you will get the same knot exactly as in this method. It is a knot that is not tied and functions equally dry or wet. Both contracts can be loosened after bearing the load. Alpine Butterfly Bend is a very respectable knot for tying almost two strings of the same diameter.

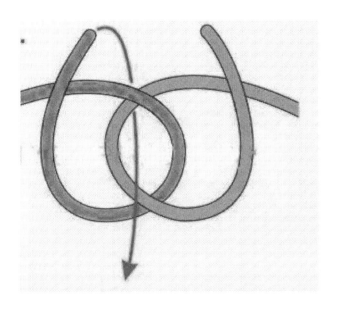

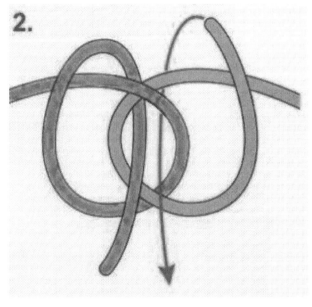

3.

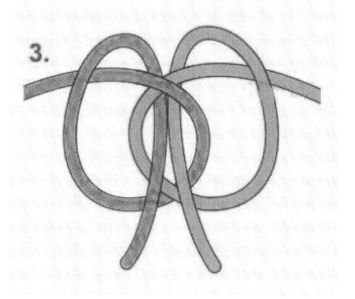

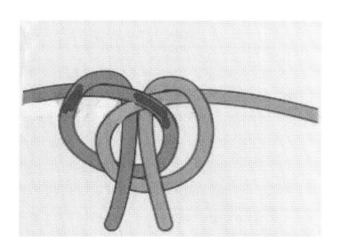

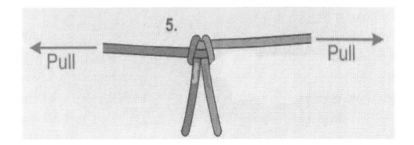

INSTRUCTIONS FOR TYING

- ✓ Form a loop over the head (the end of the action at the top of the foot line) with the rope to your left. Slide the second rope from right up through the first loop and place the end of work above your standing line (another loop from the top).
- ✓ You will now complete tying a knot over the head with the first rope, making sure to feed the end of the work through the second loop also before your loop is present, forming the knot overhand.
- ✓ Repeat the same process for the second rope.

- ✓ Tightly knit the knot over each rope until the ropes are tightened.
- ✓ Then, pull firmly in opposite directions with the lines on each rope.

ALPINE BUTTERFLY KNOT

The butterfly knot ALPINE, also known as the butterfly knot due to the shape it takes during tying, forms a secure ring in the middle of the rope. Will accommodate a load on any of the three directions independently or together. Mountaineers use the Alps to tie in the middle climber when they travel three on a rope. Also useful for making slip-resistant loops in the middle of the rope to attach carabiners to provide anchor points for other lines, an alpine butterfly is essential in boat rescue work. The knot can be utilized to isolate a damaged segment of a rope as well.

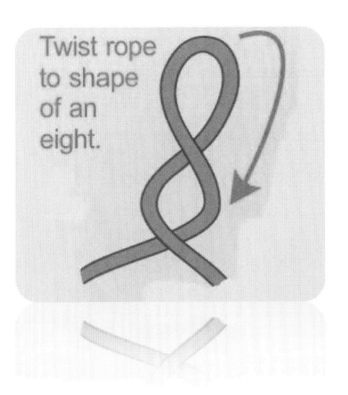

Twist rope
to shape
of an
eight.

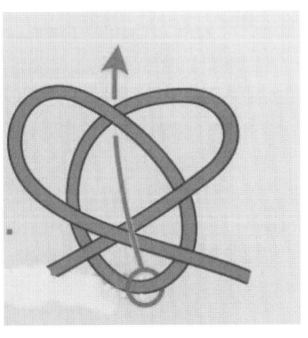

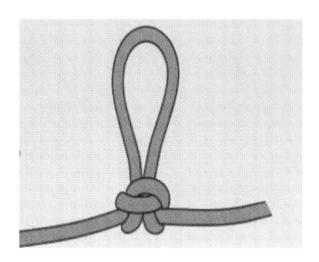

INSTRUCTIONS FOR TYING

✓ The first thing to do is to try to create a loop on the rope then spin it one full turn to create a number eight shape.

✓ Double up (Fold) the top of the eight downwards round the eight.

✓ Afterward, go up and down through the bottom opening of the eight then pull it firmly.

AUTOBLOCK KNOT

AUTOBLOCK KNOT is a quick and easy friction hitch that is usually used to support rappels. Automatic locking is often done using a temporary or factory-made ring that is held in either direction and can slip freely on the rope during the controlled descent. Most climbers now climb with a self-locking under the device, tied to a leg loop with a carabiner. This allows both hands to hold the rope under the device, providing great redundancy. Always use a self-locking (autoblock) knot on the rope as a secure backup when rappelling. However, remember that friction hitch such as self-locking will be disabled if it is jammed on the rappel device. As an additional safety measure, if the climber will hang from the device and a hitch is present for any length of time, a "lock knot" should be tied under the hitch. Tie a knot on top works well. This will ensure that in the event that something unexpected happens, the climber will not fall on the ground.

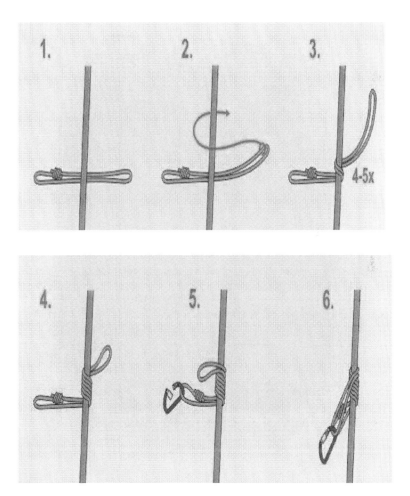

GUIDELINES

✓ Wrap the Autoblock Hitch cable four or five times around the strings of the cable. Use a thin cable such as a 5mm or 6mm fixed wire. Use most of the cord on the wrap. The more you use the rolls, the more friction will be generated.

✓ Then plug the ends of the cable into the leg lock harness loop. Close the carabiner until the cable is not released. Finally, arrange all covers to be clean and not intersect.

FARMERS KNOT

Farmer's loop knots are very useful when you want to wrap a rope away from one end of it. The loop can act as a handle or place to hold tools and other objects. You can also tie farmer's ties to loosen them in one line or isolate a bad portion of the rope. It is easy to disengage. It is similar to the alpine butterfly.

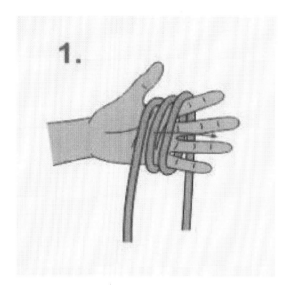

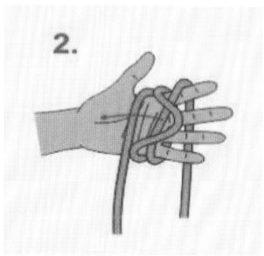

3.

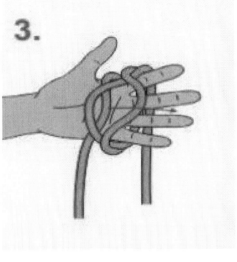

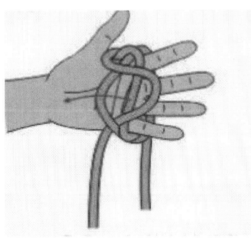

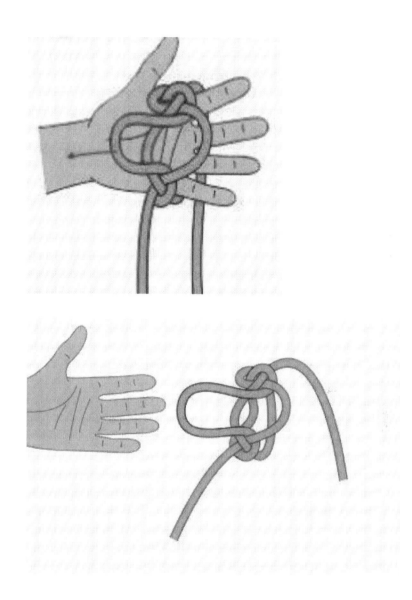

INSTRUCTIONS FOR TYING

- ✓ Start wrapping the rope around the palm of your hand three times, leaving the ends hanging.
- ✓ After that, lift the middle loop over the right loop (which becomes the middle).
- ✓ In the same way, drag the new intermediate loop over the left loop.
- ✓ Again, the half is on the right.

✓ Now in the middle on the left, and drag a little more to make the final ring the desired size.

VALDOTAIN TRESSE

"VT" Valdotain Tresse Knot is a friction knot used for the rise and fall of ropes. It is popular among arborists.

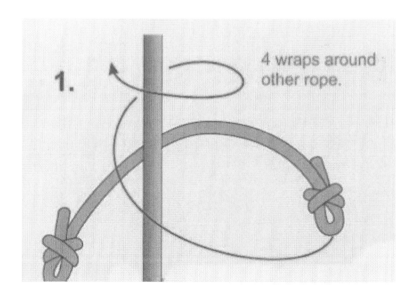

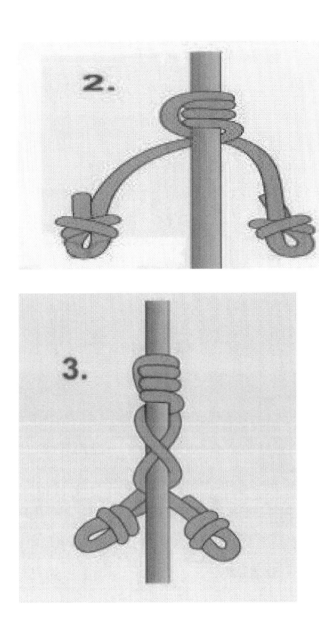

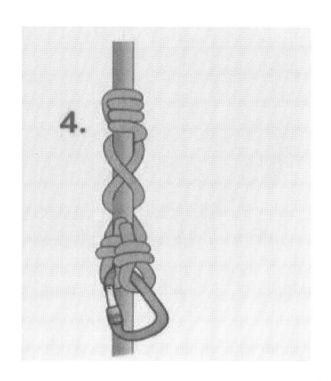

INSTRUCTIONS TO TIE THE VALDOTAIN TRESSE KNOT

✓ Make 4 turns around the main fixed rope with hand-sewn or tied prusik or split tail friction wire.

✓ After the fourth winding, lower the tails even from each other.

✓ Crossing the lines at the front then again at the back of the total 6 wraps the fixed-line.

✓ Bring the eyes in front of them and link them to a carabiner.

MUNTER HITCH

The Munter hitch provides a way to strip and land without a belaying device. This is an important knot that climbers should be aware of. It works best on large pear-shaped carabiners and should only be used with a carabiner. When installing with the Munter Hitch joint, ensure that the rope that carries the load is next to the spine of the climbing arm. Put this knot correctly, because someone's life is on the other end of the rope! This knot can cause swings or kinks in the rope.

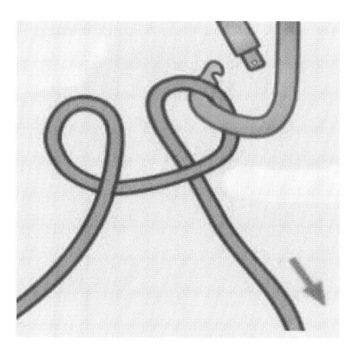

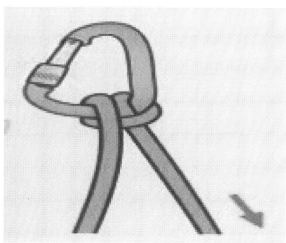

INSTRUCTIONS FOR TYING

- ✓ Create a loop on the rope and slide it into a safe climbing loop. Form a second ring with the intersection of the line versus the first ring.
- ✓ Slide the second ring onto the carabiner and close the carabiner.
- ✓ Ensure that the thread holding the load is next to the carabiner spine.

PART 5

RESCUE AND SURVIVAL KNOTS

These are the nodes that every individual must learn to tie and can be useful in urgent situations, so it would be nice to keep many of these nodes in memory. Many of these knots are very useful in knowing various purposes, such as a common whip to control strings or fibers at the end of a rope.

BACKUP NODE

Climbers often add "back knots" to their primary knot for added safety, and the backup knot makes sense in many situations involving ropes and knots. The purpose of the backup node is to prevent the primary node from loosening. There are many backup node options, for example, a simple knot over the head, but one side of the Double Hunter knot or "Half Hunter" is best. Although it consumes some ropes and is huge, it is not likely to lose them, which makes your main nodes almost certain. This version is simply one side of a double hunter tied to a long end (fifteen to eighteen inches) from the primary knot

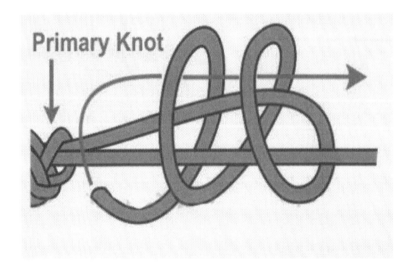

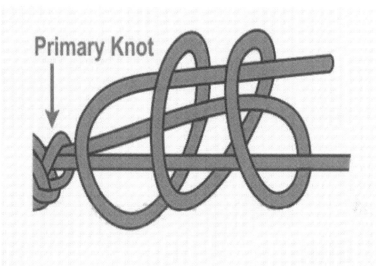

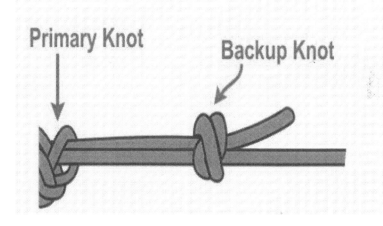

INSTRUCTIONS FOR TYING

- Wrap the free end twice around the footrope and the working part of the free end, working toward the primary knot.

- Feed the free end with the loops you just created.
- Pull the free end to tighten the back knot down on the foot line.

SPANISH BOWLINE

Spanish bowline double loop knot. The presence of double rings can be useful for light rescue operations, but care must be taken that the load on the rings is the same to avoid slipping. This is because the loops are connected to each other directly. To prevent the rings from slipping, the knot should be very narrow. Also, note that the rings can be adjusted in different sizes before the knot is fully tightened.

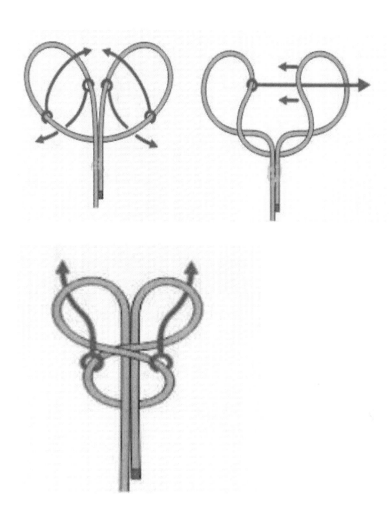

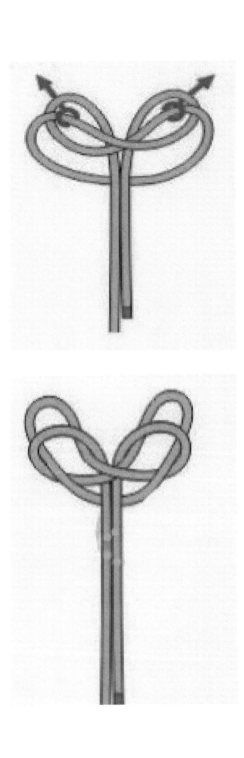

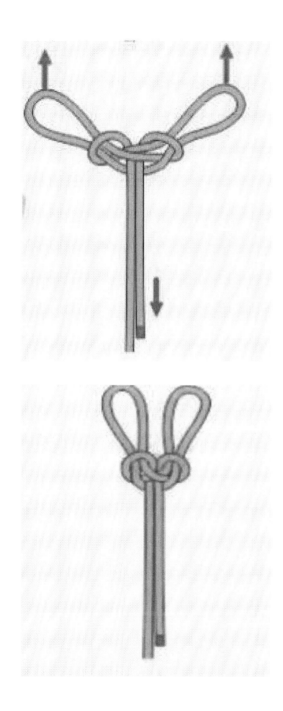

INSTRUCTIONS FOR TYING A BOWLINE KNOT

- Create a loop at the end of the rope and tuck the loop under the parallel lines. Rotate each side of the loop, toward the center, with the outer portion of the loops.
- Now take the left loop, insert it into and across the right loop, then move first under it and over the rope that crosses it.
- Grab the new small lower ring on each side and pull those sides through the top loops.
- Once the ropes reach half, pull the two vertical ropes to help tighten the knot.
- Adjust the rings and pull everything tight.

STOPPER KNOT

The stopper knot is tied to the end of a rope to prevent it from collapsing or slipping through another knot or passing again through a hole, block, or device. It makes a well trefoil-faced stopper at the end of the rope, which gives greater resistance to pulling through one of the other common sockets. Essentially, the knot is a common trope, but with the end of the rope, it passes through the eye of the rope, which closes above it.

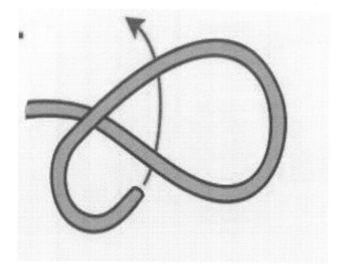

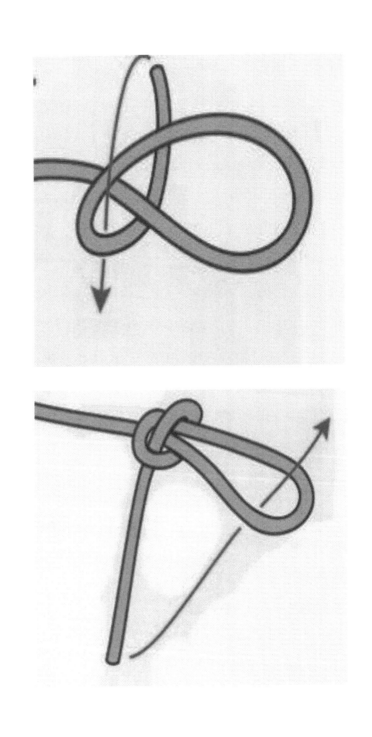

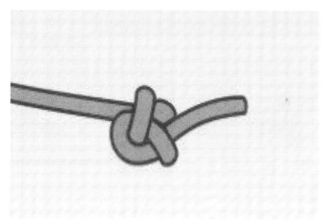

INSTRUCTIONS FOR TYING

- Form a small loop at the end of the line bypassing the end of the sticker over the permanent line.
- Tie a knot above the standing line.

- Pull the knot and tap the end of the mark by the end of the loop.
- Pull the end of the marker to the end and move the knot firmly down.
- Pull both ends tightly.

PORTUGUESE BOWLINE

This Bowline knot forms two adjustable straps. It is best to adjust the rings to fit the task in hand before tightening the knot. However, even after stretching, the rope can be pulled from one loop to another.

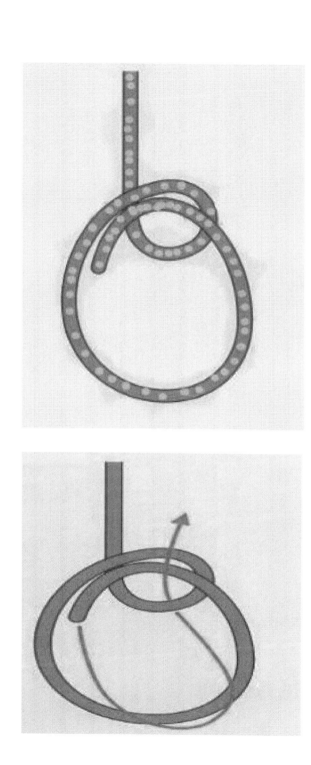

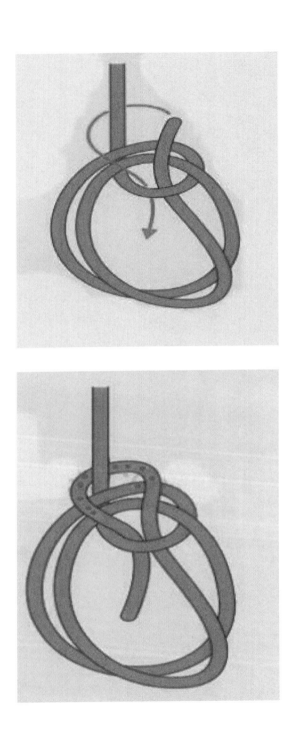

Instructions for tying a Portuguese bow knot

- Cross the end of the rope action over the foot part to form a small loop above it.
- Pinch and hold the lines.

- Now make a large episode of the required size and across the end of your activity on the small loop. Press and hold it.
- Move-in the same direction, rounding the end of the action to make the second loop,
- But this time the final action is fed through the small loop from the back.
- Slide the end of the work around the back of the standing line and back down the little loop.
- Pull the standing line and the end of the work to tie the knot.

RUNNING BOWLINE

Running Bowline produces a rope or slip ring. This can be useful for recovering objects by throwing the open-loop around it, and the loop will be tightened to the object, as the standing line tightens. The knot does not join the standing line and can be easily reversed.

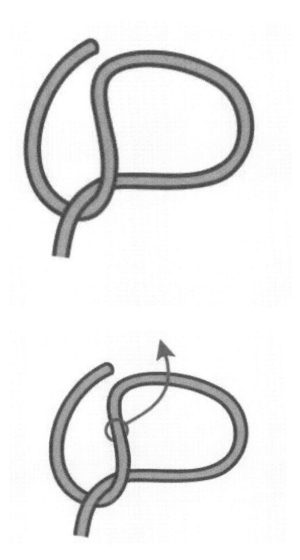

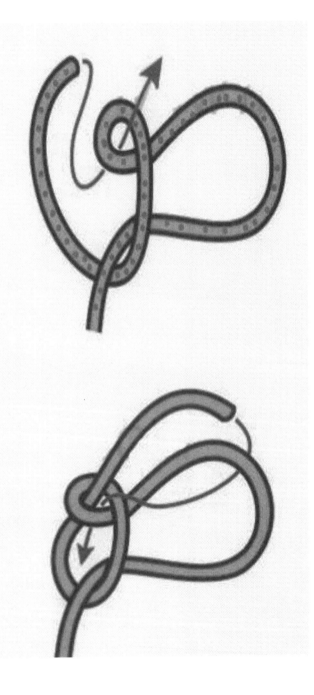

INSTRUCTIONS

❖ Double the end of the rope and wrap the end of the mark on the standing line and up to the side of the newly created ring.

❖ Create a small loop over the original loop by turning the line over itself.

❖ Feed the end of the label with a small loop.

❖ Wrap the poster end one time around the top of the large loop and then slide it back down through the small loop.

❖ Pull the end of the marker to create a fixed loop that the mainline can pass through.

Printed in Great Britain
by Amazon

72601761R00069